MW01248964

Riddle Me This!

Farmyard Riddles

Lisa Regan

WINDMILL BOOKS
NEW YORK

Published in 2015 by Windmill Books, An
Imprint of Rosen Publishing, 29 East 21st
Street, New York, NY 10010

Copyright © Arcturus Holdings Ltd.

All rights reserved. No part of this book may be
reproduced in any form without permission
in writing from the publisher, except by a
reviewer.

First Edition

Text: Lisa Regan

Illustrations: Moreno Chiacchiera
 (Beehive Illustration)

Design: Notion Design

Editor: Joe Harris

Assistant editor: Frances Evans

US editor: Joshua Shadowens

Library of Congress Cataloging-in-
Publication Data

Regan, Lisa, 1971-
 Farmyard riddles / by Lisa Regan. —
First edition.
     pages cm. — (Riddle me this!)
 Includes index.
 ISBN 978-1-4777-9161-5 (library
binding) — ISBN 978-1-4777-9162-2
(pbk.) — ISBN 978-1-4777-9163-9 (6-pack)
 1. Riddles—Juvenile. 2. Farms—
Juvenile literature. I. Title.
 PN6371.5.R46525 2015
 818'.602—dc23
                                    2013048389

Printed in the United States

SL004084US

CPSIA Compliance Information: Batch
#AS4102WM: For Further Information
contact Windmill Books, New York,
New York at 1-866-478-0556

Contents

1 True or false? There are only two "F"s in "Farmer Fuffle."

2 What is all ears and says "shhhh," but doesn't listen to a word you say?

3 A tree grows an average of 10 branches for each three feet (1 m) of height. An average branch grows 12 nuts. How many acorns would a farmer find on a chestnut tree that is 30 feet (9 m) tall?

Answers on page 28

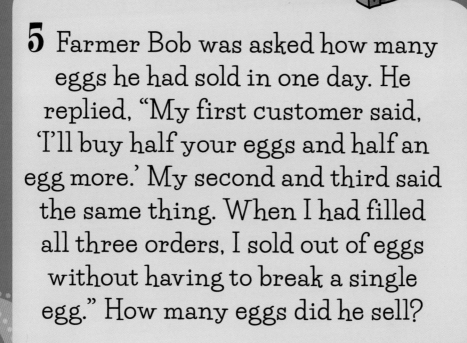

4 Which is correct: The yolk of the egg is white, or the yolk of the egg are white?

5 Farmer Bob was asked how many eggs he had sold in one day. He replied, "My first customer said, 'I'll buy half your eggs and half an egg more.' My second and third said the same thing. When I had filled all three orders, I sold out of eggs without having to break a single egg." How many eggs did he sell?

6 When is the best time to buy chicks?

Answers on page 28

7 What gets bigger, the more you take away from it?

8 In the warm months, I wear green, both during the day and at night. As it cools, I wear yellow, but during winter, I wear white. What am I?

9 The grand old nag gallops with great delight,
Then it grazes on grass and sleeps at night.
A good, strong friend for the farmer and me,
Now—how many times did you count "g"?

6

Answers on page 28

10 Mystery Word

EACH LINE OF THIS PUZZLE IS A CLUE TO A LETTER.
CAN YOU DISCOVER THE HIDDEN WORD?

My first is in chew and also in cud,
My second's in goad but isn't in good.
My third and my fourth are
letters the same,
Found in cart and in tractor,
in stock and in train.
My fifth is in lamb and in billy
but not beef.
My last is in sleep and rest and relief.
My whole can be found on a farm,
big or small.
Even when you can't see me, you'll
still know my call.

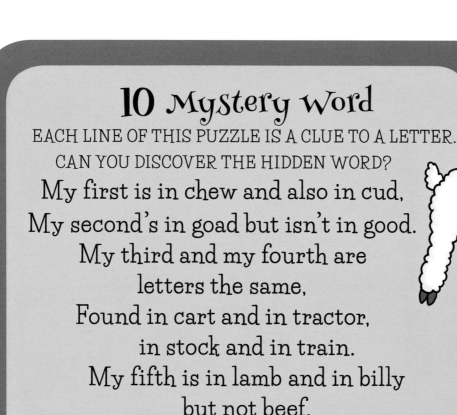

11 Where does the biggest herd of pigs live?

7

Answers on page 28

12 What has eight legs and flies?

13 I'm white and round, but I'm not always around. When the day is at its brightest, I cannot be found. What am I?

14 Farmer Sally builds three haystacks in her north field and two in her south field. Every week afterward, for five weeks, she doubles the number in the north field and adds two more in the south field. How many bales of hay will she have at the end of the harvest if she puts them all together?

8

Answers on page 28

15 Farmer Jennings was in town for the day. He went down Main Street without stopping at the red lights and turned into a street that said "NO ENTRY." A policeman waved as he went past and didn't give him a ticket or even tell him off. Why was that?

16 When is a black dog not a black dog?

17 What do you call an experienced vet?

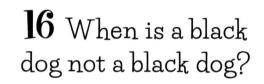

9

Whatever the weather:

18 What's written here?
BOLT
TH

19 Flowers grow upward in the warmth of summer.
This grows downward in the cold of winter.
What is it?

20 You can feel it, but you can't touch it.
You can hear it, but you can't see it.
What is it?

10

Answers on page 29

21 What flies when it is born, lies around during its lifetime, and runs when it is dead?

22 Red, purple, orange, Yellow, blue, and green. No one can touch me, Not even a queen. What am I?

23 Daisy wakes up one morning and, without getting up or opening her eyes, knows that it has been snowing. How is this possible?

11

Answers on page 29

24 What do you find in a hurricane, on a potato, and on the farmer that grows the second and sees the first coming?

25 A farmer was hard at work building a fence when a tiny thing stopped her. Although she didn't want it, she kept on looking for it. Eventually, she took it home with her because she couldn't find it. What was it?

26 What does a dog do that a person steps into?

Answers on page 29

27 Mystery Word

EACH LINE OF THIS PUZZLE IS A CLUE TO A LETTER. CAN YOU DISCOVER THE HIDDEN WORD?

My first is in goats and also in sheep,

My second's in paw but isn't in weep.

My third is in wood but isn't in grow,

My fourth's just the same as my third, don't you know.

My fifth is in bleated and cluck and in squealed,

My sixth is in stable and meadow and field.

My whole is an item you need for a horse,

Though the horse is quite happy without one, of course!

28 Read this riddle to a friend out loud: "There are 20 sick sheep in a field, and six of them have to be taken to the vet. How many are left?"

13

Answers on page 29

29 Picture a bridge 2.5 miles (4 km) long and strong enough to hold exactly 22,000 pounds (9,980 kg), but no more. A loaded truck weighing exactly 22,000 pounds drives on to the bridge. At the halfway point, a sparrow weighing 1 ounce (30 grams) lands on the truck, yet the bridge doesn't collapse. How could this be?

30 How did the farmer find his lost daughter?

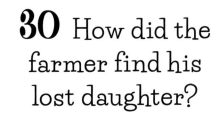

31 Most animals grow up. Which animals grow down?

14

Answers on page 29

32 Every dawn begins with me, At dusk, I'm the first thing you see, And daybreak couldn't start without What midday centers all about. All through the night, I won't be found, Yet in the dark, I'm still around. What am I?

33 Forward I am heavy, but backward I am not. What am I?

34 How would you describe a man who does not have all his fingers on his left hand?

15

Answers on page 29

35 Farmer Jones gets home after a long day harvesting. It is dark, and he is cold and hungry. He has a candle, a stove, and a fireplace but only a single match. Which should he light first?

36 I fly through the air with the greatest of ease. And I am also something you do to your peas.

37 The farmer was worried that her prize currant bush would never grow back after a cold winter. What did she say when she saw it was healthy and green?

16

Answers on page 30

38 How many bricks does it take to complete a brick barn, measuring 30 feet (9 m) by 30 feet (9 m) by 40 feet (12 m) and made completely of bricks?

39 I have six legs, four eyes, and five ears. What am I?

40 What always runs but never walks,
Often murmurs but never talks.
Has a bed but never sleeps,
Has a mouth but never eats?

17

Answers on page 30

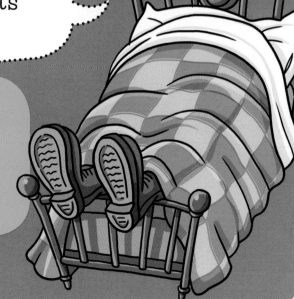

41 Farmer Jake was on one side of the river, and his trusty dog, Elmer, was on the other side. There was no bridge or boat. The farmer whistled to Elmer and shouted, "Here boy! Come on!" Elmer crossed the river, and they both walked back to the farmhouse. However, Elmer didn't get wet—how can that be?

42 What always sleeps with its shoes on?

43 What goes up and down but doesn't move?

18

Answers on page 30

44 Mystery Word

EACH LINE OF THIS PUZZLE IS A CLUE TO A LETTER.
CAN YOU DISCOVER THE HIDDEN WORD?

My first is in pickax and turnip
and spade,
My second's in blood but isn't in blade.
My third is in vegetable and also in fruit,
My fourth is in boat but never in boot.
Now write down my third again,
easy as pie,
Then end with my second, and
let out a sigh.
I have skin, I have eyes, but
still I am blind.
Can you figure out my
name from the letters
you find?

Farmyard Riddles

45 When is a
tractor not
a tractor?

19

46 If a farmer sees 13 crows at the edge of his cornfield and shoots one, how many crows will be left?

47 I have four sails, but I am no boat. I make a meal of wheat or oats. On the same spot, I'm always found, Turning around with a creaking sound.

48 Why did the farmer stand behind the angry horse?

20

Answers on page 30

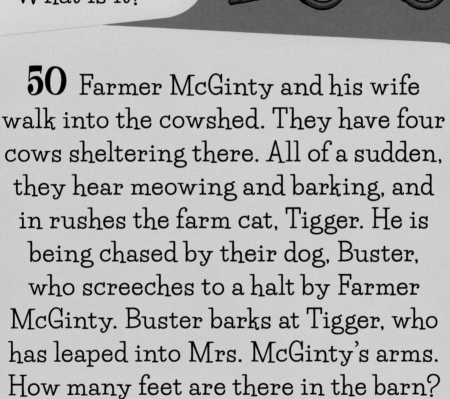

49 The more you have of it, the less you see. A box is full of it until you open the lid. What is it?

50 Farmer McGinty and his wife walk into the cowshed. They have four cows sheltering there. All of a sudden, they hear meowing and barking, and in rushes the farm cat, Tigger. He is being chased by their dog, Buster, who screeches to a halt by Farmer McGinty. Buster barks at Tigger, who has leaped into Mrs. McGinty's arms. How many feet are there in the barn?

51 What do you call a group of cattle with a sense of humor?

21

Answers on page 30

52 Farmer Molly went to market. She was selling her beautiful pies. If she sold half of them, plus half a pie, and she had two whole pies left, how many pies had she taken to market?

53 I have a little house where I live all alone. It has no doors and no windows, and if I want to go out, I must break through the wall. What am I?

54 What animal sound goes around and around a tree?

22

55 What four letters did the farmer shout at the apple thieves to frighten them away?

56 What do you call a cow that gives no milk?

57 What kind of horse has no legs?

58 Billy and Jack sneaked into the farm shop to eat their mom's homemade fudge. Billy's face ended up covered in fudge, but Jack's face was clean. Why did Jack run away to wash his face when he heard his mom approaching, while Billy stayed where he was?

23

Answers on page 31

59 A farmer raises barley in the dry season and goats all year round. What does he raise in the wet season?

60 Mystery Word

EACH LINE OF THIS PUZZLE IS A CLUE TO A LETTER.
CAN YOU DISCOVER THE HIDDEN WORD?

My first is in middle but isn't in mile,
My second's in oil but isn't in dial.
My third is in animal and barn
and in fence,
My fourth is in nickel but not bill,
dime, or pence.
My fifth is in hear and in taste
and in see,
My last is in thirty but isn't in three.
My whole is an animal that's gentle
and kind;
Pet me and stroke me—I really
won't mind.

24

Answers on page 31

61 A worm is at the bottom of a 40-inch (101-cm) hole. It crawls upward at the rate of 4 inches (10 cm) in one day, but at night, it slips back 3 inches (7.5 cm). At this rate, how long will it take the worm to crawl out of the hole?

62 What breaks but never falls, and what falls but never breaks?

63 What's more dangerous than being with a fool?

64 A rooster is perched on top of a barn. The barn has a roof that slopes to the east and the west. On which side should the farmer stand to catch eggs that roll off?

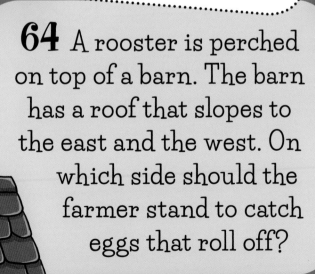

25

Answers on page 31

See how fast you can say these tongue twisters!

Mares eat oats and does eat oats.

A tricky, frisky snake with sixty superscaly stripes.

Farmer Freddy found the ferret in the farmhouse.

26

Friendly fleas and fireflies.

Six sleek swans swam swiftly southward.

If you want to buy rye, buy, if you don't want to buy rye, bye-bye!

The blue bluebird blinks.

27

Page 4

1 True—there are only two capital "F"s; the others are lower case "f."
2 A field of corn.
3 None. Acorns grow on oak trees, not chestnut trees.

Page 5

4 Neither—the yolk is yellow!
5 Seven. He sold four eggs to the first customer (half of seven is 3½ plus the other half = 4 eggs), two to the second person (half of the remaining three eggs = 1½, plus the other half = 2 eggs), and one to the third (half of the remaining egg, plus the other half = 1).
6 When they are going cheap!

Page 6

7 A hole.
8 A tree (a deciduous tree, that is!).
9 10.

Page 7

10 Cattle.
11 In a sty-scraper!

Page 8

12 Two cows in a field.
13 The Moon.
14 One!

Page 9

15 Farmer Jennings was walking through town.
16 When it's a greyhound.
17 A veteran.

Page 10

18 Thunderbolt: "th" under "bolt."

19 An icicle.

20 The wind

Page 11

21 Snow.

22 A rainbow.

23 Daisy is a cow and sleeps in a field.

Page 12

24 Eyes.

25 A splinter.

26 Pants.

Page 13

27 Saddle.

28 14. It's "20 SICK sheep," but your friend will hear "26."

Page 14

29 The truck would have burned off more than 1 ounce (30 grams) of fuel in the first mile (1.6 km) of crossing the bridge. Therefore the sparrow's weight would have no effect.

30 He tractor down!

31 Ducks or geese.

Page 15

32 The letter "d."

33 A ton. Written backward, it spells "not"!

34 Normal—it's best to have half your fingers on each hand.

Page 16
35 The match.
36 Swallow.
37 "That's a re-leaf."

Page 17
38 Just one to complete it.
39 A farmer on horseback chewing an ear of corn.
40 A river.

Page 18
41 The river is frozen.
42 A horse.
43 The temperature.

Page 19
44 Potato.
45 When it turns into a field.

Page 20
46 None—the bang of the gun will frighten away the others.
47 A windmill.
48 He thought he might get a kick out of it.

Page 21
49 Darkness.
50 Only four. The cat and dog have paws, and the cows have hooves.
51 Laughing stock.

Page 22

52 Five—she sold half (2.5) plus a half (2.5 + 0.5 = 3), so she started with 3 + 2.

53 A chick in an egg (or a butterfly in a chrysalis).

54 Bark!

Page 23

55 O I C U!

56 An udder failure.

57 A seahorse.

58 Jack, with a clean face, saw Billy's face and figured that his must be dirty, too—so his mom would know what he'd been up to. Billy could only see Jack's clean face, so he would assume that his face was also clean.

Page 24

59 His hood or his umbrella.

60 Donkey.

Page 25

61 37 days. At the end of day one, the worm would be at the 1-inch (2.5-cm) mark. At the end of the 35th day, the worm would be at the 35-inch (89-cm) mark. On the 36th day, the worm travels from 35 inches (89 cm) to 39 inches (99 cm), but it slips back to 36 inches (91 cm). On the 37th day, the worm climbs 4 inches (10 cm), which is enough for it to climb out of the hole.

62 Day breaks and night falls.

63 Fooling with a bee!

64 Neither side—roosters don't lay eggs!

Glossary

cud (KUHD) Partly digested food that an animal, such as a cow or sheep, chews in its mouth.

deciduous (deh-SIH-joo-us) A tree or shrub that loses its leaves each winter.

does (DOHZ) Female deer.

goad (GOHD) A stick used to move an animal forward; "to goad" means to provoke someone.

mares (MAIRZ) Female horses.

murmurs (MUHR-muhrz) Soft, low noises.

nag (NAG) An informal name for a horse, usually one that is old.

pickax (PIK-aks) A tool with a long wooden handle and a curved metal head.

veteran (VEH-tuh-run) Someone who has a lot of experience in a particular area of work.

Further Reading

Burbank, Lizzy. *Jokes for Kids: 299 Funny and Hilarious Clean Jokes for Kids*. North Charleston, SC: CreateSpace Independent Publishing, 2013.

National Geographic Kids. *Just Joking: 300 Hilarious Jokes, Tricky Tongue Twisters, and Ridiculous Riddles*. Des Moines, Iowa: National Geographic Society, 2012.

Websites

For web resources related to the subject of this book, go to: www. windmillbooks.com/weblinks and select this book's title.

Index